ISBN number 978-1-8382917-7-8

Contents

Hampstead Heath

Hampstead Heath is a wild park of woodland and meadows in North London. It's huge, 790 acres in fact. It's popular with Londoners of all ages as a free place to enjoy the outdoors. There are three outdoor swimming ponds (ladies', men's, mixed) as well as the Parliament Hill Lido, which is an outdoor swimming pool. The Heath even has its own police force.

Hampstead Heath exists today thanks to a long battle fought in the 1800's to protect one of the last remaining 'lungs of London'. The Heath was purchased as a public open space in 1871, on the condition that the natural state of the Heath is protected. In the same year, the UK got its first bank holiday and Londoners have enjoyed their free time on the Heath ever since.

Highlights

- Amazing architecture and stunning artwork at Kenwood House.
- Beautiful views of London from Parliament Hill - see if you can spot The Shard and St Paul's Cathedral.
- Swim in one of the outdoor swimming ponds.

Did you know...

- This park inspired the famous author C.S Lewis to write the children's stories The Chronicles of Narnia.
- Bram Stoker's book about the vampire Dracula is partly set on Hampstead Heath.
- Boudicca's Mound is a tumulus where, according to local legend, Queen Boudicca was buried after she and 10,000 Iceni warriors were defeated. However, historical drawings of the area show no other mounds other than a 17th-century windmill.

Visit Kenwood House - it's free and you can see famous artworks including Vermeer, Gainsborough and Joshua Reynolds.

Pack up a picnic, invite your friends and fly a kite on the top of Parliament Hill.

What would you most enjoy if you went to Hampstead Heath? Name some things you'd do there!

1.

2.

3.

4.

5.

6.

7.

8.

9.

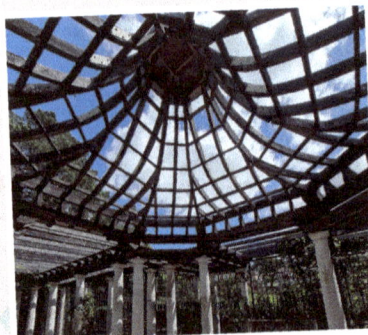

10.

Exercise

a. Horses
b. Trellis
c. Flower
d. View from Parliament Hill
e. Arches
f. Pergola
g. Pond
h. Ivy
i. Steps
j. Kite

Battersea

Battersea is a large area in South West London in the Borough of Wandsworth. It runs along the south bank of the River Thames.

One of the most iconic London landmarks is Battersea Power Station. The station was built in two separate stages, the first part in the early 1930's and the second in the early 1950s. The station was fuelled by coal and during its peak, produced a fifth of London's power.

The station was decommissioned in the 1980s and today is home to residential apartments, shops, bars and restaurants. What is most impressive about Battersea Power Station is its architecture. It makes a great impact on the London skyline, particularly with its four concrete chimneys and its brick cathedral style design. This design was popular at the time the station was built and is now one of very few examples of this style of architecture in the UK.

Every year Battersea Park hosts a fireworks show to mark Bonfire Night in early November.

Highlights

- Gaze at the cathedral-like architecture of Battersea Power Station with its four towering chimneys.
- Find some peace at the Peace Pagoda in Battersea Park.
- Spot lemurs, emus and monkeys at Battersea Zoo.

Did you know...

- Battersea Fields was a popular dueling spot.
- Battersea Dogs and Cats home has looked after 3.1 million animals since it opened in 1860.
- You might see a few helicopters in the sky, because London's busiest heliport is in Battersea.

Check out the Battersea Brewery and see beer brewing in huge vats.

If you visit the zoo at feeding time you might get to chat to a zookeeper.

Battersea Power Station burned coal to make electricity. What other ways of generating electricity are there? Are some better than others?

1.

2.

3.

4.

5.

6.

7.

8.

Exercise

a. Power station
b. River
c. Chimney
d. Peace Pagoda
e. Meerkat
f. Handrail
g. Pigeon
h. Jetty

Kensington

Kensington is in West London and is a district within the Royal Borough of Kensington and Chelsea. It is well known for its beautiful parks and museums.

In Holland Park you will find the beautiful Kyoto Garden. The Garden was opened in 1991 and was a gift from the Japanese city of Kyoto to commemorate the long friendship between Japan and Great Britain. It is a traditional Japanese garden, with tranquil waterfalls and a pond full of koi carp. There are stone lanterns and Japanese maple trees and it is home to several peacocks, which wander around the grounds.

Not too far from Holland Park is the Museum Quarter. There are many famous free museums here, including the Natural History Museum and the Victoria & Albert Museum (the V&A). The Natural History Museum exhibits a vast range of specimens including some collected by Charles Darwin. It is particularly famous for its dinosaur skeletons.

The V&A, on the other hand, has a permanent collection of over 2.27 million objects relating to art and design. The collection spans 5,000 years of art from cultures across the world. It also has some of the largest collections of ceramics, glass, textiles, costumes, furniture, sculptures, drawings and photography in the world.

Approximately a 20 minute walk away from the V&A you will find Kensington Palace. Beside the palace is Kensington Gardens, including the Italian Gardens and a beautiful water garden which was a gift to Queen Victoria from her husband Prince Albert.

Did you know...

- Queen Victoria was born in Kensington Palace.
- Prince William and his family lived at Kensington Palace until they moved to Windsor Castle in 2022. It remains their official London residence.
- The Natural History Museum welcomes around four million visitors every year.

Pick one of the free museums to explore.

Enjoy the tranquility of Kyoto Garden.

Museums display things people go to look at. These can be about different themes (Science, History, The Natural World). What things would you put in your museum?

1.

2.

3.

4.

5.

6.

7.

8.

9.

10.

Exercise

a. V&A Museum
b. Royal Albert Hall
c. Science Museum
d. Natural History Museum
e. Kyoto Garden waterfall
f. The Earth
g. Beak
h. Road sign
i. Geese
j. Dinosaur skeleton

Camden

Camden is an area of North London, famous for its market, culture and fashion. For many years, it has been a haven for people on the outskirts of mainstream society, such as punks. Camden Market is one of the most famous markets in London, maybe even the whole of England. The market started in the 1970s and has grown into a hub of creativity. You will find stalls selling handmade clothes and jewellery, music memorabilia, art and so much more. There are also food stalls that sell cuisine from all over the world.

The market sits alongside Camden Lock on The Regent's Canal. The canal begins at the River Thames, and joins the Grand Union Canal which finishes in Birmingham, over 130 miles away. Each year, 28 million visitors come to the market. Camden resident and singer Amy Winehouse worked at the market, and previous residents include singers Mick Jagger, Bob Dylan, David Bowie and many more. Just a few minutes walk away is Regent's Park, one of London's eight Royal Parks, where there is a boating lake and an open air theatre.

You can also walk to Primrose Hill which is the next park, and has stunning views over all of London. It also contains a tree planted in 1864 to mark the 300th anniversary of Shakespeare's birth.

Highlights

- Grab some food from one of the stalls in Camden Market and sit on the edge of the canal to eat.
- Walk to the top of Primrose Hill and get a photo of the London skyline.
- Listen to some live music from buskers in Camden.

Did you know...

- The zoo is not allowed to contain elephants because it is built within a city.
- Many years ago, duels were fought on Primrose Hill.
- The musician Prince once had a store near Camden Market.

Shelter inside Camden Market and browse many of the fascinating stalls selling everything from teapots to circus equipment.

In the summer smell the roses in Regent's Park.

If you had a market stall, what would you sell on it?

1.

2.

3.

4.

5.

6.

7.

8.

9.

Exercise

a. Canal
b. Cobblestones
c. Padlocks
d. Lock
e. Prints
f. Market
g. Street
h. Boot
i. Shops
j. Street art
k. Sweets

10.

11.

Brick Lane

Brick Lane is a street in the East End of London. It got its name from the brick kilns that were located there, which were used to rebuild the city after the Great Fire of London. For many years immigrants have settled around Brick Lane. From French Huguenots in the 17th century, to Irish immigrants, Ashkenazi Jews and, most recently, the Bangladeshi community. This has led to the current influx of curry houses which you will find on the street. In the last 30 years, Brick Lane has become well known within the art student population and there are now modern bars and pubs that nestle between the curry houses.

To the north, you have Shoreditch, which has become a centre for young creatives and trendsetters. There are many quirky pubs and bars here too. To the west you have Spitalfields Market, where many of the newly arrived residents sold their handmade crafts to the market. Now there are independent traders selling cutting-edge fashion, interior design items and food.

To the south, you have Whitechapel. In the 19th century, this area of London suffered from huge poverty and overcrowding and was notorious for the crimes of serial killer Jack the Ripper.

Highlights

- The Brick Lane Mosque reflects the history of the people living in the area. It was first a church then a synagogue and now the Brick Lane Jamme Masjid.
- Wander around Spitalfields Market and see the various independent stalls.
- Haggle for the price of a curry in one of the many Brick Lane restaurants.

Did you know...

- You can see graffiti art in Brick Lane from the likes of Banksy. The area has also been used for many music videos.
- From the 1950s to 1970s there was an animal market from Club Row to Sclater Street. It sold many types of animals including lion cubs!
- Some of Shakespeare's first plays were performed in a theatre in Shoreditch and a memorial to Elizabethan actors can still be seen in Shoreditch Church.

Follow in the footsteps of Pablo Picasso and Frida Kahlo, by visiting Whitechapel Gallery which is free of charge.

Grab a drink and sit on the rooftop of Shoreditch Boxpark, soaking up the local culture and watching the world go by.

Brick Lane is like a lot of London. It has changed over the last few years. Think of some of the ways that buildings can be used. What kinds of buildings have you seen used for new purposes?

1.

2.

3.

4.

5.

6.

7.

8.

9.

10.

Exercise

a. One way street
b. Church
c. Elephant
d. Security camera
e. Market Entrance
f. Art work on a shutter
g. Clothes rails
h. Floral decoration
i. Festoon lights
j. Graffiti

City of London

The City of London is a historic financial district, home to the London Stock Exchange and the Bank of England. It is now home to many skyscrapers that tower above the medieval alleyways.

At the heart of the area is St Paul's Cathedral. It hosted the funerals of Admiral Nelson, the Duke of Wellington and Winston Churchill, and the wedding of Prince Charles and Lady Diana.

Walking north from St Paul's, you head towards the Barbican Centre. On the way is Postman's Park. In 1900 it became the location for a memorial dedicated to self-sacrifice, and contains the names of ordinary people who died whilst saving lives.

The Barbican Centre is the largest performing arts centre in Europe. It hosts music concerts, theatre performances, film screenings and exhibitions. It is home to the London Symphony Orchestra and the Royal Shakespeare Company. Some areas are free to walk around.

The Museum of London at West Smithfiled, documents the history of the capital from prehistoric times to now. It contains over six million objects and it's totally free to visit.

Highlights

- Book free tickets to go up to the Sky Garden, which is at the top of one of the City of London's skyscrapers, to see fantastic views of the capital.
- Walk around St Paul's Cathedral and learn about the UK's most famous church.
- Spend some time in Postman's Park reading about the heroic sacrifices many have made over the years.

Did you know...

- St Paul's sits on Ludgate Hill, which is the highest point in the City of London.
- The remains of the original Roman city wall, the edge of the oldest part of London are located to the north of the Tower of London.
- St Mary-le-Bow church is the church mentioned in the nursery rhyme "Oranges and Lemons". Traditionally, people who are born within earshot of the church bells are considered to be "Cockney" (someone from The East of London).

**The City of London is the business district, with some very tall buildings.
What do you think of tall buildings in a city?
How do you think they make people feel?**

1.

2.

3.

4.

5.

6.

7.

8.

9.

10.

Exercise

a. St Paul's Cathedral
b. Information board
c. The Barbican Centre
d. Sculpture
e. Globe
f. Ruins
g. Pond
h. Bus
i. Dome
j. Hose pipe

Westminster

Westminster is the centre for British government. On the banks of the Thames are the Houses of Parliament (officially called the Palace of Westminster), which serves as the meeting place for politicians including the Prime Minister. Big Ben is the famous clock that towers over the palace and is visible for miles around. Opposite the Houses of Parliament lies Westminster Abbey, the location for many coronations of British Royal Family. It is also the burial site for monarchs, prime ministers, actors, scientists and other famous people from history. Walk north from the Houses of Parliament up Whitehall, and you will pass statues and memorials such as Sir Winston Churchill, the Cenotaph and the Suffragettes. You will also find ten Downing Street, the home of the Prime Minister. You will often see groups of people protesting outside the gates to the street.

Continuing up Whitehall, on your left you will see the Horse Guards building guarded by two soldiers of The King's Life Guard who are posted outside from 10:00am to 4:00pm daily. Behind the building is Horse Guards Parade where you can see the Changing of the Guard and of in Trooping of the Colour ceremonies.

At the end of Whitehall is Trafalgar Square. This public space contains Nelson's Column, guarded by four lion statues. Huge fountains stand beneath the column. The National Gallery art museum sits on the square and houses over 2,000 paintings. Entry to the main collection is free of charge.

Highlights

- Walk around some of the most iconic buildings in British politics.
- Soak up the atmosphere and people watch in Trafalgar Square.
- Visit the free collection of paintings at the National Gallery.

Wander around the National Gallery and view paintings from the likes of Da Vinci, Constable, Rembrandt, Van Gogh, Monet, Caravaggio and many more.

Spot statues in Parliament Square and remember people and events from Britain's past.

Did you know...

- Big Ben is actually the name of the bell that sits within the clock. However, most people refer to the clock and the tower by the same name
- 10 Downing Street is over 300 years old and contains around 100 rooms
- The northwest plinth in Trafalgar Square is known as "The Fourth Plinth", and is a public art commission. This means that various different sculptures and other artistic installations have appeared there over the years.

In the UK we have a Prime Minister, not a President, and a small number of political parties, with elections every five years. How does this differ from other countries?

1.

2.

3.

4.

5.

6.

7.

8.

Exercise

a. Bus
b. Sign
c. Suffragette
d. Gate
e. Westminster Abbey
f. Horse Guard
g. Winston Churchill
h. Elizabeth Tower/Big Ben

St James's

Start at Admiralty Arch and walk up The Mall towards Buckingham Palace. The Mall plays an important part in ceremonies as well as Royal events such as weddings and funerals.

You will pass St James's Palace on your right, and the Diana Princess of Wales Memorial Walk on your left in St James's Park. Also on your right is Clarence House where King Charles III and Camilla, Queen Consort live.

Buckingham Palace is the King's official London residence and has served as the official London residence of the reigning monarch since 1837. It has 775 rooms, including 19 State rooms, 52 Royal and guest bedrooms, 188 staff bedrooms, 92 offices and 78 bathrooms.

Next to Buckingham Palace is St St James's Park which is currently home to six pelicans. Pelicans were first introduced to the park in 1664 as a gift from the Russian Ambassador, with over 40 pelicans making the park home since then. They are free to roam but rarely go far from the lake. Look out for them catching fish from the lake and swimming and preening together.

Highlights

- Watch the pelicans being fed fresh fish between 2:30pm and 3:00pm every day, next to Duck Island Cottage.
- Recreate the last stretch of the London Marathon by running up The Mall.
- Spot a friendly squirrel in St James's Park.

Explore the free collection of Art at the Royal Academy of Art.

Plan a picnic in St James's Park.

Did you know…

- If the King's royal standard flag is raised above the palace then the King is currently in residence. When the Union Jack flag is flown the King is elsewhere.
- If you look at the lamp posts along this road you will see they each have a ship at the top. These are meant to be Nelson's fleet of ships which he looks down on from his column in Trafalgar Square.
- Pelicans are outgoing, sociable creatures. One mischievous pelican used to fly over to London Zoo in Regent's Park to steal fish for lunch and they will often sit on park benches next to visitors!

**The King is our Head of State (we don't elect a president!).
What do you know about the King, and his family?**

1.

2.

3.

4.

5.

6.

7.

8.

9.

10.

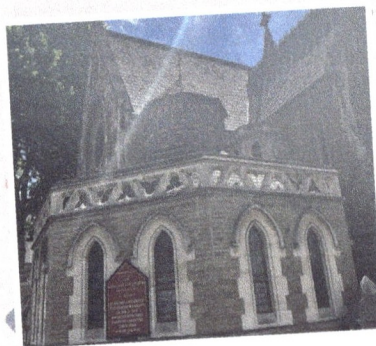

11.

Exercise

a. Buckingham Palace
b. The Mall
c. Pelican
d. Flag
e. Algae
f. Lamp post
g. Statue
h. Police car
i. Shadow
j. Lion
k. Crown
l. Black Cab (Taxi)
m. Window Frame

12.

13.

King's Cross

Start at King's Cross Station, one of London's major travel hubs and home of Harry Potter's platform 9¾. Stop for a picture at platform 9¾ and then visit Regent's Canal.

On the banks of Regent's Canal is Granary Square, home to the famous Central St Martins Art College. The Square has over 1,000 fountains. Walk over to the beautiful St Pancras station, built in 1868, which is also home of the Eurostar, the train which connects Great Britain with Europe.

Behind St Pancras, on the site of the former goods yard, is the British Library. It is the national library of the UK and one of the largest libraries in the world.

Visit old St Pancras Church and the Hardy Tree, where gravestones surround the trunk. When St Pancras and King's Cross stations were built they dug up parts of the graveyard which then had to be tidied up afterwards. The gravestones were arranged around the trunk of the tree, in an everlasting hug.

Highlights

- Watch the changing fountains in Granary Square.
- Walk along the towpath of The Regent's Canal. You can walk all the way to Camden Market and beyond.
- Look out for art installations around King's Cross, you can even see art students at work in Central St Martins.

Visit the public areas of Central St Martins Art College.

Relax on the grassy seating on the banks of The Regent's Canal and watch the boats go by.

Did you know...

- The canal was built so barges could unload their cargo of coal, grain and other goods for the City of London. It was so cold in the winter of 1962/63 that Regent's Canal froze over so no cargo could move on it for weeks. By the time the ice thawed, most of the freight traffic was using roads, never to return to the canal.
- Before poet and novelist Thomas Hardy was famous, he worked as an apprentice and tidied up the graveyard at St Pancras Church, allegedly coming across the body of a two headed man.
- King's Cross was previously known as Battle Bridge after a Roman battle with Queen Boudicca and the Iceni tribe in 61 AD.

Do you think people will be using trains in 100 years?
What do you think will be the main transport of the future?

1.

2.

3.

4.

5.

6.

7.

8.

9.

10.

11.

Exercise

a. Train
b. Clock Tower
c. Station entrance
d. Platform 9¾
e. Hedge
f. Underground sign
g. Canal and Barge
h. Stairs
i. St Pancras Sign
j. Library books
k. Arched roof

Stratford & Canary Wharf

Stratford in East London has become best known for the 2012 Olympics, held at the Olympic Stadium in the Queen Elizabeth Olympic Park. Today Stratford is home to many busy locations including sporting venues, housing and Westfield shopping centre, all thanks to the London Olympics.

The Queen Elizabeth Olympic Park is 560 acres. You can find people sunbathing in the meadows, children playing on the playground in the pleasure gardens, and joggers and walkers strolling along the canals of the River Lea. The Olympic Park website provides free trail guides to help spend your day at the park. Try not to get wet in the labyrinth like fountain! At sunset, head to the top of the slope by Tumbling Bay Playground to see the Shard light up.

If you like modern architecture head over to Canary Wharf just 30 minutes away by bus or Docklands Light Railway (DLR). Canary Wharf was built in the 20th century and is part of the London Docklands. It is home to the financial district, including one of the most impressive buildings in London, One Canada Square. Here you can gaze in awe at large shiny skyscrapers, stroll through roof gardens, visit free museums and relax in public squares.

There are plenty of free things to do and see in Canary Wharf. The Museum of London Docklands provides a history of London and water trading. It is located in a former port warehouse, open seven days a week. Crossrail Gardens, in Crossrail Place is a wonderful alternative to the Sky Garden. There is no need to book in advance for this rooftop garden, with various pop-up art installations. From here, you can walk to Jubilee Park, full of fountains, art, waterways and statues.

Highlights

- Canary Wharf hosts free art all throughout the area.
- Fancy a farm day in the city? Head over to Mudchute Farm.
- Learn about the history of the docklands at the Museum of London Docklands.

Did you know...

- Did you know that Stratford was known as Straet Forda, which meant a ford (river crossing) on a Roman road? This is because Stratford lay next to a ford on the road from Colchester to London.
- Did you know the ArcelorMittal Orbit, built as an observation tower for the 2012 Olympics, is now a slide?
- British Iraqi architect Zaha Hadid designed the London Aquatic Centre.

How many Olympic sports can you name?

1.

2.

3.

4.

5.

6.

7.

8.

9.

10.

Exercise

a. Orbital slide
b. Skyscrapers
c. Aquatic centre
d. Stadium
e. Train track
f. Towpath
g. One Canada Square
h. Traffic light
i. Cityscape
j. Station

Greenwich

Greenwich is one of four World Heritage Sites in London. It is known for giving its name to the Meridian line, Greenwich Mean Time as well as its maritime history. It was home to Henry VIII, Elizabeth I and The Royal Naval College. The Royal Naval College today is now home to the National Maritime Museum. It was home to Henry VIII, Elizabeth I and The Royal Naval College, which now houses the National Maritime Museum. The Museum focuses on British naval history and how navigation at sea has impacted Britain today.

In the 20th century, the Cutty Sark, a National Historic Clipper Ship, was placed next to the riverfront and is a popular landmark. It was the fastest tea clipper of her time. Located in Greenwich is one of the best-known parks in London, Greenwich Park. It was formerly a royal hunting ground. There is a beautiful rose garden at the top of the 163-acre park.

You can walk through the Greenwich Foot Tunnel to cross the River Thames. It was opened in 1902 because ferries were sometimes unreliable. The entrance of the foot tunnel starts near the Cutty Sark and ends across the Thames at Island Gardens in Canary Wharf.

Highlights

- Explore the free galleries of The Maritime Museum.
- Visit the Queen's House to see the Armada Portrait of Queen Elizabeth I.
- See the best view of London in Greenwich Park from the top of the hill.

Did you know...

- After dark, in Greenwich Park, you can see the symbolic green laser that beams along the Prime Meridian.
- At 1:00pm exactly every day of the week the bright red time ball drops at the Royal Observatory on top of Flamstead House. This was a public signal of the time to ships on the Thames.
- The Royal Naval College has been used as backdrops in many movies: Les Misérables, Four Weddings and a Funeral, Pirates of the Caribbean 4, The King's Speech, and more.

Visit the free astronomy centre to answer all your questions about space.

Walk along the Thames path and learn about the Thames Barrier, which stops London from flooding.

What do you know about the solar system?

1.

2.

3.

4.

5.

6.

7.

8.

9.

10.

Exercise

a. Foot tunnel entrance
b. Royal Naval College
c. Sunset
d. River Thames
e. Columns
f. Forest
g. Clock Tower
h. Roses
i. Windows
j. Ship
k. Railings
l. Parkland

11.

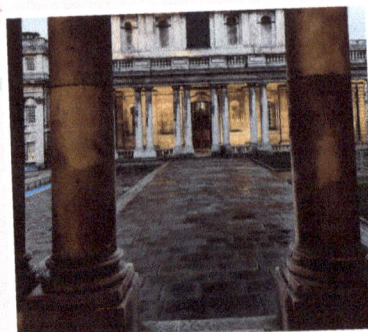

12.

Southbank

The Southbank of the Thames used to be marshland but it was in the 1800s that The Southbank started to develop. In 1951 the Festival of Britain regenerated the areaand and brought people from all over the United Kingdom to visit. Along the river you can find art, food markets, landmarks and green spaces to relax. This is the perfect area for a stroll along the River Thames.

The London Eye is a great starting point for a day out. Watch skateboarders take over the Undercroft which is full of graffiti and has been part of London's skate scene for 40 years. Why not move on to The Tate Modern for some more modern-day art, located in the former Bankside Power Station. When it first opened to the public, there was just a small display of British artworks. Today, there are nearly 70,000 artworks. This museum is free and could take an entire day to see everything. Next to the Tate Modern is Shakespeare's Globe, a world-renowned theatre and cultural landmark. This is a reconstruction of the original Globe Theatre which was destroyed by fire. To end the River Thames tour of the South Bank you can cross over the iconic Tower Bridge. This beautiful blue bridge was opened in 1894. Tower Bridge is a 'bascule' bridge which can be raised to allow taller ships through. Bascule means seesaw.

Highlights

- The top floor of the Switch House at Tate Modern has a free viewing terrace with London skyline views and a view of the dome of St Paul's Cathedral.
- Leake Street Graffiti Tunnel located near the London Eye.
- Tower Bridge raises. Schedule is available online.

Did you know...

- The London Eye was previously known as the Millennium Wheel
- The architect of the Bankside Power Station (today Tate Modern), is the designer of the red telephone boxes around London.
- In 1952, the number 78 bus, had to jump from one bascule to the other, as the bridge began to rise while being driven by Albert Gunter.

Be inspired by modern art in the Tate Modern.

Enjoy the street performers of the Southbank.

What is your favourite kind of art?

1.

2.

3.

4.

5.

6.

7.

8.

9.

10.

11.

12.

Exercise

a. Fountain
b. Phone Box
c. Palm Tree
d. Tate Modern
e. Riverboat
f. Walkway
g. Skateboarder
h. London Eye
i. Hungerford Footbridge/
   Golden Jubilee Bridge
j. Bikes
k. Bush
l. Merry-go-round

www.ingramcontent.com/pod-product-compliance
Lightning Source LLC
Chambersburg PA
CBHW040909100426
42737CB00050B/3494